LIFE IN THE RAINFOREST

Edward P. Ortleb

Primary Science Resource Guide
Includes Transparencies, Reproducibles, and Teacher's Guide

LIFE IN THE RAINFOREST

Contributing Author: Ann C. Edmonds
Illustrations: Donald O'Connor, Maggie Rechtiene
Cover Design: E. Rohne Rudder
Managing Editor: Kathleen Hilmes
Editors: Beth Parada, Kelly Morris

Copyright © 1997
Milliken Publishing Company
1100 Research Blvd.
St. Louis, MO 63132
All rights reserved.

Cover photo reprinted courtesy of NASA.

To the Teacher

*But if you stay long enough inside the jungle and allow yourself
to become atuned to its rhythms, you will probably come to the
conclusion that the jungle is more than the sum of its vegetation
and its animals; it is a living, pulsing entity.*

Ivan Sanderson, <u>Book of Great Jungles</u>

The rainforest ecosystem is a fascinating and rewarding area for you and your class to study.
The colors, sounds, and smells of the rainforest will stimulate the imagination, while the study
of its ecosystems will fulfill science, social studies, math, and language arts core objectives. The
rainforest offers the chance to explore the scientific concepts of the water cycle, the food chain,
adaptation, and conservation, and inspires learning in both local and exotic ecosystems. Skills
emphasized in this course of study include observation, prediction, classification, and
conclusion–making.

The information contained in this resource and activity book follows a learning cycle that
includes: a) **free exploration** by the students; b) **expansion of exploration** through activities that
allow children to test, integrate, and sort out their discoveries; and c) **application of concepts**
through individual and group projects which provide students with the opportunity to enhance
and share what they have learned.

Each section includes teacher resource material, planned lessons, and expansion activities.
Students will examine various items, books, and resources. The display table's contents of fruits,
nuts, woods, and other rainforest items will pique students' interest. Books and other reference
materials will both stimulate reading and writing skills and encourage learning. Perhaps the class
will be most fascinated with the plants, the animals and peoples, or the future of the rainforest.
Guided by the students, the teacher can choose which of the activities to use.

In the **Application/Presentation** section, students concentrate on a particular subject within the
rainforest ecosystem. Individual reports, a grand mural, letters to conservation organizations,
and a play are some of the avenues for consolidating the learning from the previous two
sections. The teacher facilitates the learning process as the students prepare for their own
teaching. A culminating activity gives the class the opportunity to share their learning with
others.

A **To the Parent** reproducible page gives a brief explanation of the unit and suggests ways
parents can enhance or share some of the children's activities and discoveries.

Four **reproducible** pages are included for students to record observations and discoveries. They
are referenced as **R** within the text.

Four **transparencies** actively engage students in recording, discussion, or interpretive activities.
They are referenced as **T** within the text. (See also inside front and back covers.)

A **bibliography** includes books and resources for children and teachers.

Contents

To the Parent

Welcome to the rainforest! We are preparing to study the rainforest ecosystem. Rainforests constitute only two percent of the earth's surface, but they are vital habitats. We will be studying the locations, importance, and diversity of the rainforest ecosystem. We will also be studying what we can do to help preserve the rainforest. So much of our lives is connected to these wet forests. Please help us with our study.

Help your child collect material for recyclable art: milk jugs, egg cartons, scrap paper, newspapers, and other odds and ends to make an interesting mural collage. Each child will make a miniature jungle. Please send in one empty, clean, two–liter plastic bottle with cap. A note will be sent home when these or other materials are needed.

Look around the house with your child for rainforest products. Here are just a few: rubber, balsa wood, mahogany, avocado, banana, guava, papaya, grapefruit, orange, lemon, lime, mango, passion fruit, pepper, pineapple, cinnamon, chocolate, allspice, cloves, ginger, mace, paprika, vanilla, macadamia nuts, tapioca, tea, coffee, cashews, Brazil nuts, coconut and palm oils, and chicle (in chewing gum). Discuss how you use these items. Imagine how your lives would be different without them. Find out how they got to your home from so far away.

Visit a zoo or botanical garden to see the living treasures of the rainforest. Talk about the need to be more careful with our natural resources and what your family can do to help.

Enjoy your exploring!

Getting Started

Tropical rainforests once covered the earth around the equator. Plants, insects, reptiles, amphibians, birds, and other living things thrive in these damp, warm ecosystems. Vast and fragile, the rainforest is vital to human needs and vulnerable to human greed. This resource book will help you and your class discover what is in the rainforest, why the rainforest is endangered, and what can be done to help preserve it.

Free Exploration

Begin your course of study by discovering what your students know about the rainforest from books, television, or parents. Let them share their knowledge and build upon it through the suggestions below.

1) During the **free exploration** segment, set up a **display and discovery area** highlighting items originating from the rainforest. Include different household items. (See *To the Parent* (**R**) for a list.)

2) **Add a globe** so that the children can see where the rainforests grow.

3) **Collect** books, magazines, photographs, maps, and other reference materials on the rainforest.

4) **Bring in rainforest plants** like croton, caladium, rubber plant (Figus), or philodendron. The children can begin to investigate the different types of leaves and stems.

5) Try to arrange a trip to a local **botanical garden** or **zoo** to introduce children to some of the plants and animals of the rainforest. Students' questions, comments, and insights during the trip can help shape the focus of additional activities to pursue in the classroom.

The children will begin to focus on specific areas such as mammals, the predator–prey cycle, and the role of people in the rainforest during free exploration. In this part of the learning cycle, the teacher is a watcher and listener, noticing curiosity and motivation. As you talk and learn with your students, decide where the rainforest unit will focus in the **expansion activities** and **application of concepts** sections. Throughout free exploration, make note of the words that students use to describe the rainforest environment. Keep a list of these descriptive words to use in later activities.

Keeping Records

1) Each child will keep a **rainforest log.** Provide time during the free exploration period for making entries. Use the **reproducible pages (R)** included in this book as recording devices. Younger students may dictate journal entries to the teacher or draw pictures as their entries. Initial journal entries may be very simple, amounting to no more than a descriptive word, phrase, or drawing. As the school year progresses, recording should become more sophisticated. The journals will give the teacher a sense of what the children want to learn and give the students a personal record of the unit.

2) Provide students with individual **portfolios** in which they can save drawings, reproducible pages, written work, and other materials pertinent to their study of the rainforest. Decorate the cover with a tissue–paper collage to capture the diversity of texture and color in the rainforest. Cut bright colors from magazines into rainforest shapes, or draw favorite rainforest animals to make a simple cover.

3) Create a **class book** about the rainforest on chart paper. Report regularly by adding new words, asking and answering questions, and listing and classifying rainforest creatures, smells, sounds, and concepts. Hang the charts on the classroom walls, or connect the papers with a ring.

Vocabulary

Introduce new concepts to the students through vocabulary words. These are not words that students need to learn to spell, but should be familiar to them by sight and sound. Have students illustrate new words in their journals. Vocabulary words are **boldfaced** when they are first introduced in the text.

adaptation: a characteristic of an organism that helps it survive in its habitat

bromeliad: a special epiphyte with stiff, tightly curled leaves of red and green; the cone–shaped center fills with water, which acts as home and breeding ground for insects and amphibians

buttress: a structure on the trunk that supports rainforest trees and prevents them from falling over easily

cacao: (or *cocoa*) a tropical plant whose beans are made into cocoa powder or chocolate

canopy: an upper layer of plants in the rainforest; only the emergents are taller

consumer: an animal that feeds on plants or other animals

decomposer: an organism that causes the decay of complex organic materials into simpler compounds; bacteria, yeasts, molds, and fungi are all decomposers

deforestation: burning, flooding, cutting down all the trees; leads to severe erosion of the land

drip tip leaf: common type of rainforest leaf; the tip is tapered and points down, causing water to drip off the plant

emergent: layer of rainforest vegetation comprised of the tallest trees that protrude through the canopy

epiphyte: a plant that grows on tree branches using aerial roots to absorb water and nutrients from its surroundings (examples: orchids and some types of mosses, ferns, and bromeliads)

food chain: the linear relationship between predator and prey

food web: a network of interrelated food chains

forest floor: the ground surface of the rainforest that is covered by organic debris which quickly decays

herb: a vegetation layer in the rainforest that is often not well defined; includes plants a meter or less in height

humidity: moisture in the air; rainforests usually have high humidity

jaguar: a large member of the cat family with a spotted coat; an example of a predator

kapok tree: a large tree, often called an apartment house because it is home to many creatures; kapok is a useful insulating material

liana: a thick, climbing vine found in the rainforest

orchid: an epiphyte plant with colorful flowers often having one of the petals forming a liplike structure

predator: an organism that feeds on other organisms; usually refers to a carnivore

prey: an organism that is eaten by another organism

producer: a green plant that is capable of manufacturing its own food

rainforest: a woodland area with large amounts of rain and often warm temperatures

shrub: the layer of plants that range from five to ten meters in height

terrarium: a glass–sided enclosure such as an aquarium used as a habitat for terrestrial plants and animals

understory: layer of vegetation in the rainforest below the canopy; trees here range in height from 15 to 20 m

water cycle: the continuous and cyclical process of water evaporation, condensation, and precipitation

The Rainforest: *Where Is It? What Is It?*

Teacher Information

A **rainforest** is generally defined as a tropical, evergreen, broad–leaved woodland which receives over 200 cm (80 in.) of rain each year. Rainforests are most commonly found in the low altitude zones near the equator where the climate is hot and wet year–round. Rainforests are found in three major areas on our planet: 1) Central and South America, 2) central and western Africa and Madagascar, and 3) southeast Asia/New Guinea. Tropical rainforests are often referred to as jungles. This is a derivation of a Hindu word used to describe a dense, tangled growth of vegetation.

Location... The largest contiguous aggregate of rainforest is found in the Amazon and Orinoco river basins in South America. Segments of the New World jungle are found in northwestern South America, throughout Central America, and into southern Mexico. In Africa, the rainforest occupies portions of central and western Africa (the Congo, Niger, and Zambezi river basins) and Madagascar. About one–fourth of rainforest acreage is located in southeastern Asia, the East Indies, and the Malay Archipelago.

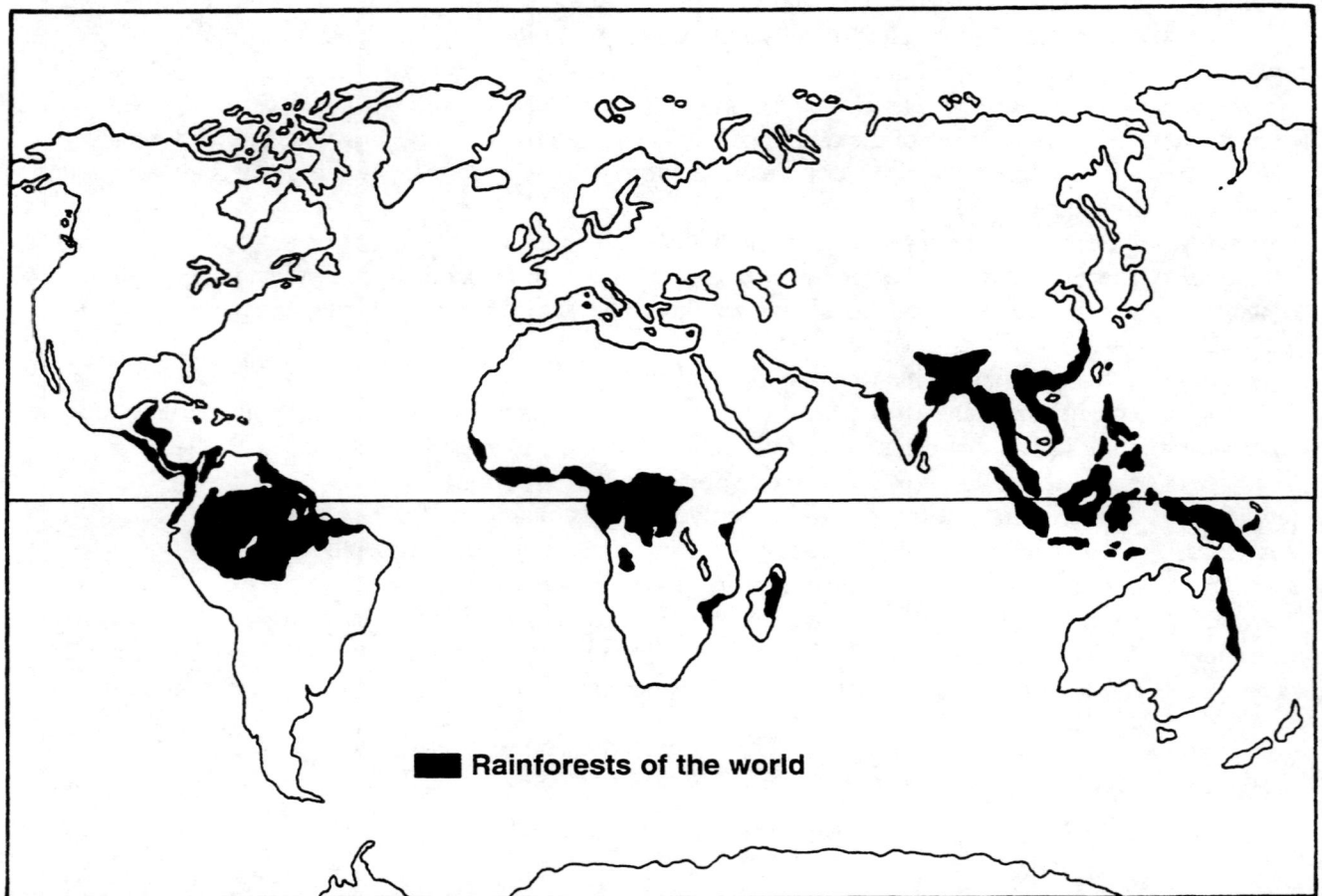

■ Rainforests of the world

Types of Rainforests . . . The most widely known type of rainforests are the **tropical rainforests** described above. However, there are other forests that receive an abundance of rain, but have different climatic conditions and/or geographical locations. **Monsoon forests** in India, Bangladesh, Burma, Thailand, and Sulawesi (an island of Indonesia) are characterized by a very dry season and a very wet season. Extremely heavy rains are experienced from April to September. **Montane rainforests** exist in the lower to mid elevations of mountainous tropical areas. The trees here tend to be less tall as a consequence of the lower temperatures. **Cloud forests** are found on certain mountain summits that have an almost perpetual layer of mist. Often they are the habitat of numerous amphibians. Puerto Rico and Costa Rica have excellent cloud forest wildlife preserves. **Tropical scrub forests** are located in areas that have a longer, drier season than the tropical rainforests, such as western India, Pakistan, western Mexico, and western Argentina. **Tropical deciduous forests** are found in China and eastern Australia. Rainfall in these forests is slightly less than in tropical rainforests and is unevenly distributed. This results in smaller, hardwood deciduous trees being the prime vegetation. An unusual rainforest is found on the west coast of the state of Washington. Average rainfall is over 350 cm (140 in.) a year. The forest floor, tree trunks, and tree branches are festooned with mosses and ferns.

Climate . . . Tropical rainforests are characterized by a warm, annual mean temperature that has little variation daily or monthly, high **humidity,** and heavy rainfall. The mean annual temperature is approximately 27° C (81° F), whether in Panama, Brazil, Nigeria, or Burma. The monthly variation is less than that between night and day. Annual rainfall is about 200–400 cm (80–160 in.).

Living Things . . . The combination of constant warmth and moisture promotes luxuriant plant growth in the rainforest. Animal life is also abundant. A mature tropical rainforest has a greater diversity and variation of plant and animal species than found in any other biome.

Expansion Activities

The following activities give students the opportunity to study maps and to learn about the physical characteristics of the rainforest.

Activity 1: Mapping the Rainforests

materials: world map or globe, *Rainforests of the World* (T), *Rainforests of the World* (R)

Use a world map or globe to show students where the rainforests stand. Leave the globe on the science table for them to continue exploring. Show *Rainforests of the World* (T) and hand out *Rainforests of the World* (R) for students to color in where the rainforests are located today. Encourage older students to label the continents and countries which contain tropical rainforests. Place the completed maps in individual portfolios.

Going Further: Find out where the rainforests are being destroyed. Circle these areas on the maps used in *Activity 1*. Discuss why the rainforests are disappearing. What happens to the animals?

Activity 2: Building a Rainforest Vocabulary

materials: colored markers, tagboard or chart paper

Read out loud the list of vocabulary words you noted during the free exploration period described on page 6. Ask the students what other words they might use to describe the rainforest to someone. Write both the new and the old words on tagboard or chart paper with a colored marker. Have students use the vocabulary words to develop descriptive sentences about the rainforest. Students may record their sentences in their rainforest logs. If you like, this is also a good time to introduce the vocabulary words listed on page 7.

Activity 3: Taking a Guided Imagery Tour

One way children can envision the rainforest environment is by listening to a story about an imaginary walk through the rainforest. To make the story vivid, include several of the adjectives and rainforest descriptions children have suggested (*Activity 2* above). Embellish with your own ideas. Below is an example of a guided imagery story set in the rainforest. Ask students to keep their eyes closed as they listen to the story. Play rainforest music softly in the background to help set the mood. The story introduces students to rainforest features such as light, shade, warm temperatures, humidity, and sounds.

You and several of your friends decide to take a trip to a tropical rainforest. For this trip you pack a long–sleeved shirt, pants, socks, a pair of boots, a hat, and a raincoat. After a long plane ride, you arrive at your destination. The first thing you notice is how warm and humid the air feels. Your group takes a short bus ride to the beginning of the trail that leads into the rainforest. By now your shirt is wet and sticking to your skin. The backpack holding your raincoat feels uncomfortable. A guide is waiting to take you into the jungle, and you and your friends step from the sunlight onto the dark, jungle trail. The many layers of trees above you block out most of the sunlight. Someone screams! Something is moving on a tree next to the trail. You laugh—it is only a lizard chasing a beetle. Then everyone looks up into the trees. What is that noise? Your guide has a pair of binoculars. She looks up and sees a brightly colored bird with a large beak. "It's a toucan," she explains. "I wonder what made it squawk like that?" Several children yell that they see some animals moving in the tree branches. Someone says that the animals look like big spiders. You notice that they have long tails which they use to move through the trees. It is a band of spider monkeys. They are jumping from tree to tree looking for something to eat. Suddenly the rainforest becomes even darker. Thunder fills your ears. Along with the thunder comes a terrible howling sound. Everyone is frightened. Could it be a jaguar? Your guide assures you that it is not a jaguar, but a band of howler monkeys. They often howl with the thunder. It is time to get out your raincoat and hat because it is starting to rain. Wow, what a rain! One of your friends shouts that he has seen a little bug–eyed monster. Everyone rushes over to the spot and they see a beautiful, green tree frog with bright red eyes. With a couple of jumps it leaps away into the jungle. As quickly as the rain started, it stops. Beautiful, shiny blue butterflies flutter by. Across the trail hundreds of ants march in a line. Each one has a piece of green leaf in its jaws. These are leaf–cutter ants carrying the pieces of leaves to an underground home. Mold will grow on the leaves and the ants will eat the mold. What a day this has been in the jungle. There is so much to see. Tomorrow will be another exciting day in the jungle!

Rainforest Log: Enter a short story of what your group might see on a second day walking through the jungle.

10

Activity 4: Light in the Rainforest

materials: construction paper, scissors, masking tape, 30 x 30 cm (12 x 12 in.) piece of cardboard, thermometer, extension cord lamp

Construct rainforest tree models of various heights and widths using construction paper. A cylinder of construction paper serves as the trunk and a flat piece of paper represents the leaf mass. Attach the two pieces together with masking tape to form a tree. Attach the trees to the cardboard base with tape. Suspend an extension cord lamp about 15 cm (6 in.) above the "forest." Note the bright "sunlight" over the forest top and the shade underneath. How does the amount of light compare? Take the temperature of the upper surface of the jungle canopy and of the floor of the forest. What is the temperature at the top? At the bottom? Why might some animals like to live on the floor of the rainforest?

Rainforest Log: Enter observations, discoveries, or impressions in words, sentences, or drawings.

Activity 5: Rainforest Soils

materials: a heavy aluminum foil pan with depth of about 5 to 7 cm (2 to 3 in.), clay soil, organic soil, water

Fill the pan three–fourths full of clay soil and cover with a 1 cm (½ in.) layer of organic soil. Tilt the pan by placing a thick book under one end of the pan.

Pour one cup of water into the raised portion of the pan. Observe what happens to the water in the pan. Have students relate this to jungle soils that have been eroded and to those that have not been eroded. How do rainforest trees help prevent erosion? Where does the organic matter on the jungle floor come from?

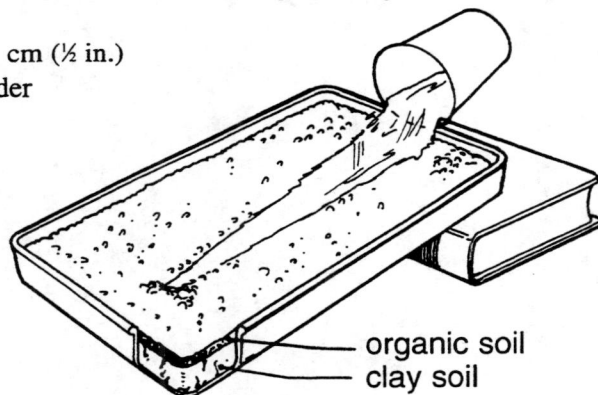

organic soil
clay soil

Rainforest Log: Enter observations, discoveries, or impressions in words, sentences, or drawings.

Going Further

1) Students can write a description of a rainforest that is not a tropical rainforest. Tell how it is the same as and yet different from a tropical rainforest.

2) Encourage students to use their rainforest logs to ask questions and propose their own answers. For example: Who lives in the rainforest? What does the rainforest smell like?

3) As a class, make a graph (or graphs) comparing the monthly average temperature and rainfall in your area with that of the rainforest. Have students record the results in their rainforest logs.

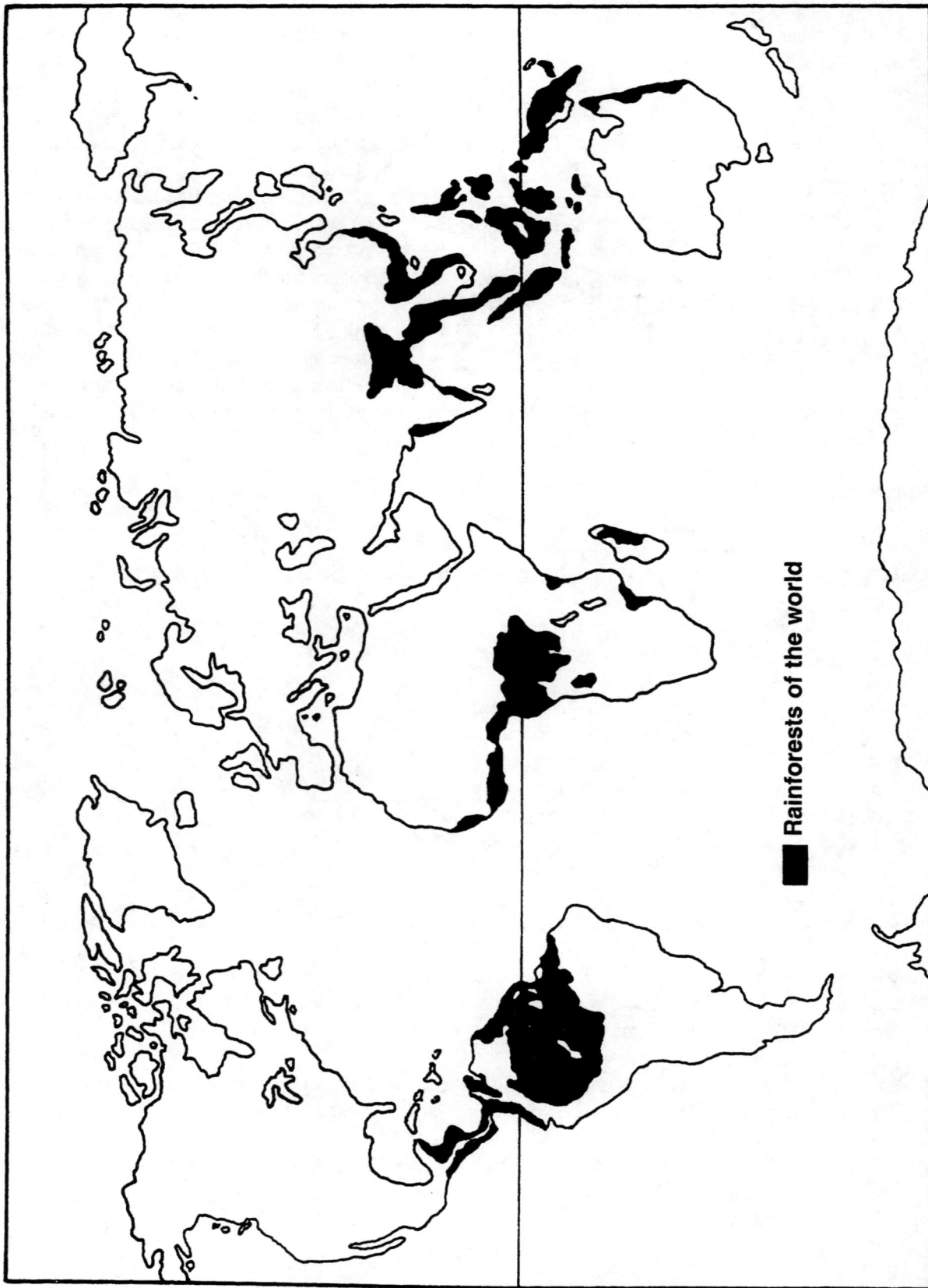

Name

Rainforests of the World

■ **Rainforests of the world**

Name

Where Are the Rainforests?

Where are the rainforests of the world? Draw them on the map below.

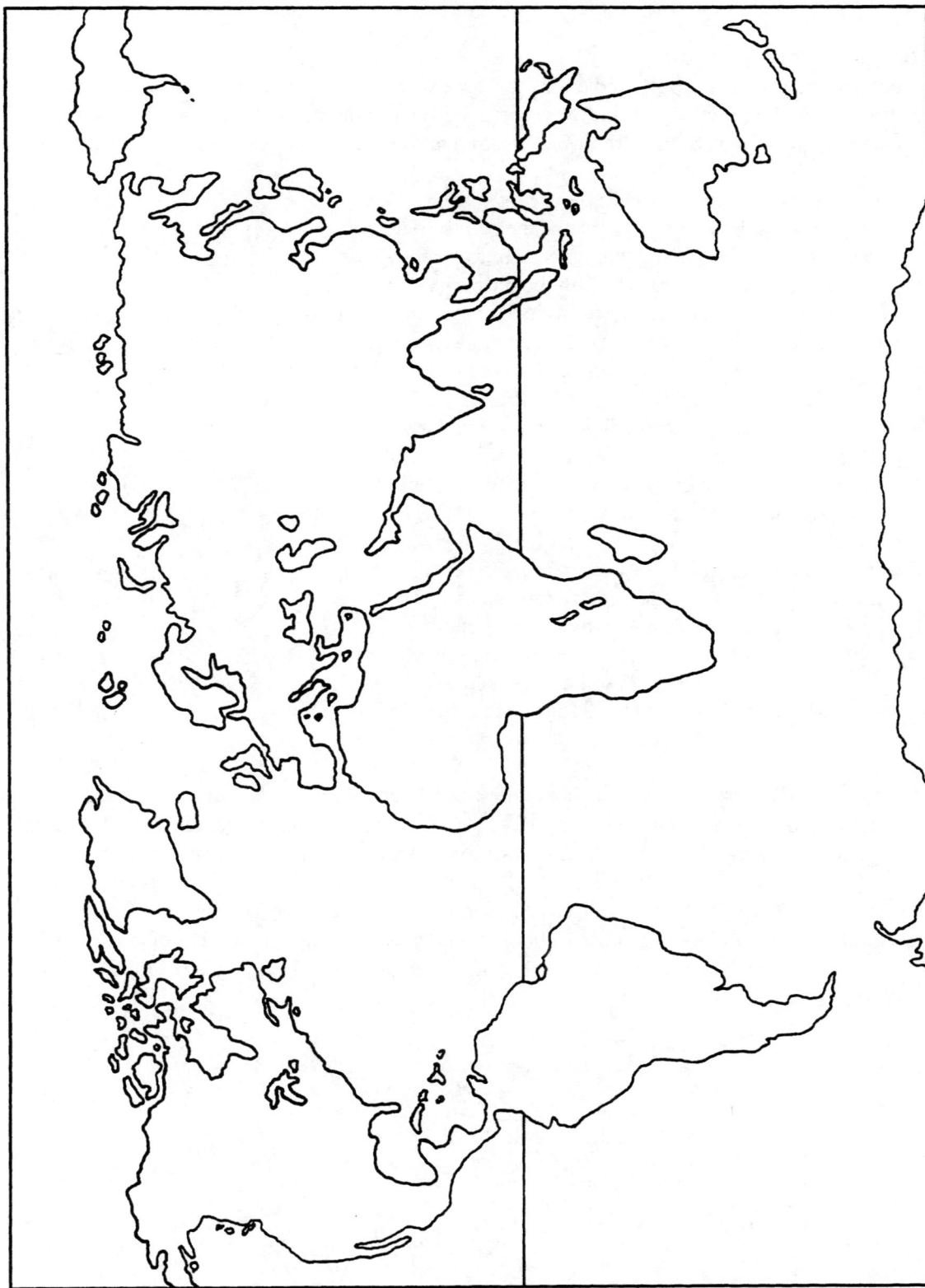

Life in the Rainforest

Plants of the Rainforest

Teacher Information

Rainforest plants are complex and colorful. These plants often have fruits, flowers, buds, and old and new leaves—all at the same time. Rainforest plants have the same parts as all plants—leaves, stems, and roots—but possess unique **adaptations** to the wet, dim, and nutrient–poor environment they inhabit.

Roots . . . Rainforest trees have shallow root systems. Water and nutrients lie near the surface of the soil, so deep root systems are not required. Many trees are top–heavy with masses of leaves and would easily be blown over in a storm. Such trees may have stilt roots that grow out from the base of the tree trunk, providing extra support. Some trees have aerial roots that dangle from branches to the ground, supplying extra water and nutrients. **Epiphytes**, such as **orchids** and **bromeliads**, have roots that anchor the plant to a tree branch. They obtain moisture and nutrients needed from the air and from bits of soil and debris on the branches.

Stems . . . The stems and trunks of some rainforest plants are not as solid as those of temperate forest plants. Their hollow insides provide a habitat for many kinds of animals. However, they are subject to being blown over. **Buttress**–like structures on some trees help to support the weight and height of the tree. **Lianas** and other vines tie some trees together in a mutual support system.

Leaves . . . Rainforest plants display an interesting variety of leaves: sharp, pointed palm leaves; wide philodendron leaves; furry leaves, like those of our house violets; metallic brown or polka–dotted leaves; smooth or spiky leaves. Many rainforest leaves have "**drip tips**" so that precious rainwater can drip from layer to layer, following the leaf troughs. This prevents water from accumulating on the leaf and accelerating its decay. The tight spiral arrangement of long, thin leaves such as those of the pineapple family form a central cone that fills with water. This pool of water is home to a number of insects and amphibians. Tree, bush, and vine leaves come in a variety of shades of green—the evidence of the chlorophyll necessary for photosynthesis.

Flowers and Seeds ... All plants depend on water, sunlight, and nutrients in order to survive. They need to be able to produce seeds to ensure the propagation of the species. Unique shapes, colors, and smells help plants compete for resources. Without wind and water to help disperse seeds, plants must depend on insects, birds, and other animals. The flashy colors and intricate blossoms of orchids attract insects and further pollination. The sweet–smelling odors of some flowers attract bees and other insects to feed on the nectar or pollen and thereby help pollinate the plants. Some plants such as rafflesia (which has the largest flower in the world) have foul odors that attract flesh–eating insects and thus pollinate the species. The seeds of some plants are very tasty and are chewed on or eaten by animals; the discarded or digested remains can produce a new plant in a new location.

Layering of Rainforest Vegetation ... The rainforest, with its bountiful rainfall and warm temperatures, provides a stable environment which gives rise to an incredibly complex ecosystem. The plant community is layered, or stratified. The tallest trees may be more than 50 meters (165 feet) in height and are called **emergents**. These giants of the jungle protrude above the canopy layer. The **canopy** plants reach about 35 meters (115 feet) above the jungle floor and form an umbrella–like covering. Below the canopy is an additional layer of **understory** trees ranging in height from 15 to 20 meters (50 to 65 feet). The **shrub** layer is not well–defined and includes those plants that are 5 to 10 meters (16 to 32 feet) tall. The **herb** layer is most often missing due to the dense shade at the 1–meter (3–foot) height. There is insufficient sunlight here for most types of plants to grow. The **forest floor** is covered with the debris of fallen plant materials and animal remains. Decomposers rapidly change complex organic compounds into simpler ones. This rich organic material supplies nutrients for the entire plant community.

Products of the Rainforest ... The tropical rainforest is a veritable treasure chest of foods, woods, minerals, and medicines. Governments, both foreign and native, are anxious to use the rainforest. Corporations are interested in rainforest treasures such as fine woods like mahogany and teak, and in gold buried beneath the thin layer of soil. Businesses are interested in using the land to raise cattle more cheaply than in North America. Plantations of rubber trees, bananas, and pineapples provide work, and therefore food and shelter, for many more people than the rainforest itself could support. Unfortunately, due to erosion, the farms and ranches will help only briefly. Soon the rains will wash away the soil.

Over a quarter of our daily medicines already come from the rainforest. These can be harvested without destroying large tracts of land. Curare, used in poison–arrow hunting, is now used to treat multiple sclerosis. Scientists have also found that the Madagascar periwinkle relieves the effects of some cancers. The rainforest has been called an unexplored medicine chest. Scientists are eagerly researching new possibilities to cure disease and to ease pain.

Life in the Rainforest

There are many optimistic plans to farm rainforest areas carefully so that both erosion and tribal destruction are minimized. One approach is called extractive farming. Cashews, Brazil nuts, chocolate (**cacao** beans), eggplants, lemons, papayas, pineapples, some teas and coffees, bananas, peanuts, cassava (tapioca), and potatoes are some of the foods already being harvested in the rainforest today. Palm trees are grown and their leaves harvested for making roofs and woven hats; palm oils are used to make soaps, paints, and perfumes. Rubber has been tapped from rainforest trees for over 100 years. A substitute for fossil fuels has also been discovered in the rainforest: the Brazilian copaiba sap, which is used in place of diesel fuel. Carefully nurtured, the rainforest can produce for humans as well as for its own ecosystem. We can create sustainable crops—not just crops that tear apart the ecosystem.

Expansion Activities

The following activities provide opportunities for students to learn about parts of rainforest plants. They also begin a continuing series of activities which contribute to the three–dimensional mural activity in *Application of Concepts: Making Connections* (see page 28).

Activity 1: A Jungle Plant

materials: cup for each child, pothos or philodendron plant, scissors, potting soil

Some of our common houseplants originally grew naturally in the dim and moist environment of the rainforest. Arrange some potted plants in the classroom rainforest display area. Students can easily root or propagate a new plant from a leaf. The cutting should include the node and a leaf. Put the cutting in water and watch the root grow. When the root is about 5 cm (2 in.) long, plant it in some soil. Pothos and philodendron plants are excellent for this activity.

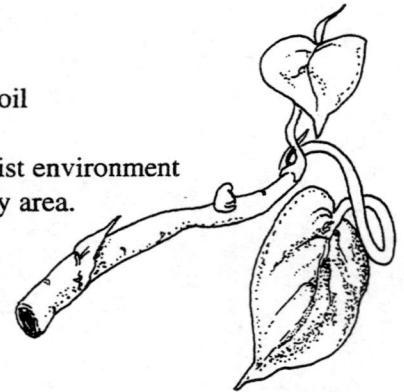

Activity 2: Studying Bromeliads

materials: top of pineapple with leaves, flower pot, liquid measuring device, potting soil, sand, water, plastic bag

Grow a pineapple plant to observe the characteristics of bromeliads, a family of tropical plants. Use a liquid measuring device (measuring cup or graduated cylinder) to determine how much water the whorled–leaf top can hold. What kinds of animals could live in this miniature jungle pond? Why would the water stay in this pond and not dry up?

Slice off the leafy top from a fresh pineapple, including about 3 cm (1 in.) of the fleshy fruit. Let dry for two days. Fill a 4–inch pot with potting soil to within 3 cm (1 in.) of the top. Moisten the soil and pack it into the pot. Sprinkle a ½ cm (¼ in.) layer of sand over the soil. Place the pineapple top onto the sandy surface and then cover the fleshy part with more potting soil. Cover the plant and pot with a plastic bag and place the entire assembly in a warm, shady area.

When roots appear in about 8 to 10 weeks, remove the plastic bag. Replant the pineapple in a 5– or 6–inch pot. Study the leaves and roots of this bromeliad plant.

Going Further:

1) Make a bromeliad. Cut ovals of stiff construction paper. Staple into a thick circle, leaving a center. Draw the pop–eyed tree frog or the tiny, poisonous, yellow or bright blue frogs and put them into the bromeliad pond or onto the leaves. Save the bromeliads to add to the three–dimensional mural. (See *Application of Concepts: Making Connections.*)

2) Make liana vine leaves for the mural. Take long paper sheets (newspaper or construction paper). Roll the sheets tightly to make the stems. Paint with green poster paint. Cut out oval leaves from construction paper and tape or staple them onto the stems. Students can also draw insects or snakes traveling on the vine. For quick and simple vines, have students cut construction paper into long vine shapes.

Activity 3: Making a Terrarium

materials: clean, plastic, two–liter soda bottles with caps; bean, carrot, and radish seeds; other vegetable or flower seeds; potting soil; water

One way to show your class the rainforest **water cycle** is to make individual **terrariums.** These miniature jungles can also be used to study the layering of rainforests. Make a few extra bottles for class experiments to illustrate the effects of light, water, and erosion.

1) Add about 8 cm (3 in.) of potting soil to the bottom of clean, plastic, two–liter soda bottles with caps.

2) Add carrot seeds to simulate palms and ferns.

3) Add bean seeds to represent the emergent trees or lianas. Radish plants will look like broad–leaf understory plants. Add other vegetable or flower seeds with approximately the same growing times to show the possible diversity of plants in a small area of forest.

4) Add about ¼ cup of water to each bottle and seal tightly.

5) Place the jungle terrariums on a window sill and watch the water cycle begin. The children can see the evaporation/condensation cycle almost immediately as the temperature within the bottles rises and falls. When the plants begin to grow, students will be able to see the transpiration/condensation cycle of the rainforest.

6) Experiment with putting the bottles in different places. Note that the plants need sunlight. Like rainforest plants, the bottle plants will compete for sunlight and space. Direct sunlight may increase the temperature within the bottle and affect the growth of the plants.

Going Further:

1) Keep one terrarium for an extended period to show the effects of overcrowding.
2) Remove the top of another bottle to show what happens when the water cycle is broken.
3) Poke a hole in the bottom of one bottle. Add 8 cm (3 in.) of potting soil. Place the bottle in a pie pan. Keep pouring water into the bottle. What happens to the dirt when there are no plants to hold it?
4) When the rainforest unit is over, the children can plant the seedlings outside where they will have more room to thrive.

Rainforest Log: Keep an individual or class journal reporting on plant growth and water cycle patterns, posing and answering questions about why and how it works. Adding words to written and spoken vocabulary are ways to integrate the learning the children do every day.

Activity 4: Exploring Tropical Nuts and Fruits

materials: shelled peanuts, Brazil nuts, cashews, nutcracker, banana, pineapple, papaya, star fruit, paper towels, knife, paper plates

Prepare a tray of nuts. Examine, compare, and contrast the cashew, peanut, and Brazil nut shells. Explain that the Brazil and cashew nuts grow on trees and that peanuts grow underground. Discuss how a seed's shell must protect the seed and yet be ready to open when the environmental conditions are favorable. In cracking nuts, note the complexity of the Brazil nut and the simplicity of the peanut. Take apart a banana, papaya, pineapple, star fruit, or other rainforest fruit. Compare the color, texture, and shape of each. Discuss what part of the plant is eaten. For example, the banana is the fruit, the sugar cane is the stem, the cassava (tapioca) is the root. Note how each fruit seed is different. Organize in order of size. Can you even find a banana seed? Compare with the seeds of cashews and Brazil nuts.

Activity 5: Where Do Spices Come From?

Spices obtained from rainforest products have been used to flavor foods for hundreds of years. Europeans fought wars and braved oceans to find peppercorn to flavor and preserve, cinnamon and nutmeg to flavor their meals, and sugar to sweeten foods.

materials: grater, nutmeg, mace, allspice, cinnamon, ginger root, cloves, vanilla (bean and liquid extract), magnifying glass

1) Grate the nutmeg meats to produce dark flecks of nutmeg. Compare these flecks of nutmeg with the mace, which comes from the dried external fibrous covering of the nutmeg. In the jungle, the toucan spreads the powdery mace and then drops the harder, cracked nutmeg seed. Note the odor of both.
2) Grate the cinnamon bark. Again compare with the powdered variety. Is the change from solid to powder a physical or chemical change? Note the odor.
3) Grate the ginger root. Skin the rhizome and then squeeze out the juicy particles. Is this a physical or chemical change? Note the odor.

4) Examine a vanilla bean. Feel its slippery surface and smell its rich odor. Compare with vanilla extract.

5) Cloves are the flowers of the clove tree. They were highly prized as meat and fruit preservatives. Examine with a magnifying glass. Can you see the flower? Note the odor.

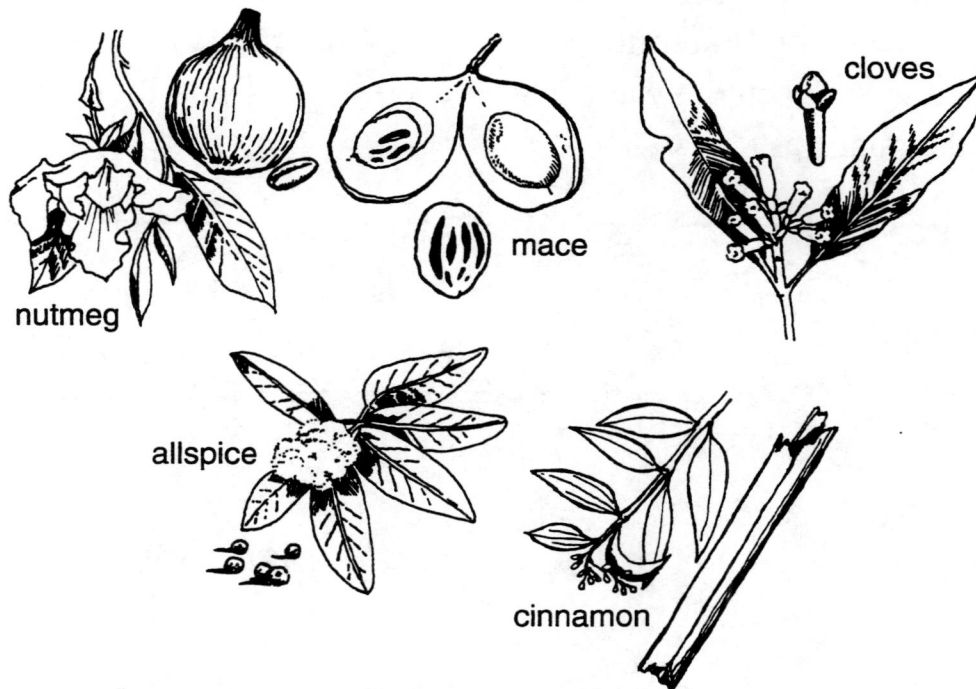

Rainforest Log:

1) Have students write the name of each spice and explain what part of the plant it comes from. For example, cinnamon—bark; ginger—rhizome; mace and nutmeg—nutmeg seed; cloves—flowers; vanilla—bean or seedpod.

2) Keep an individual or class journal reporting on plant growth and water cycle patterns, posing and answering questions about why and how it works. Add words to written and spoken vocabulary to integrate the learning. Students can write how plants have developed certain adaptations to compete for survival in the rainforest ecosystem. For example, epiphytes have aerial roots in order to obtain the water and nutrients they need, since they are not in contact with the forest soil.

Layers of the Rainforest

Scientists divide the rainforest into five layers. Label the **Forest Floor**, the **Shrub Layer**, the **Understory Layer**, the **Canopy Layer**, and the **Emergent Layer**. Then draw and color the creatures found in the different layers of the rainforest.

Animals of the Rainforest

Teacher Information

The rainforest abounds with visual and auditory delights. The brilliant colors of toucans and parrots, delicate butterflies, and brightly patterned snakes and amphibians all demonstrate the active competition for survival. The damp odors of decaying vegetation are mixed with fragrant odors of tropical flowers. The sounds of howler monkeys, crickets, growling **jaguars**, and rain dripping through layers of foliage fill the jungle. Many animals are adapted for life in one of the vegetation layers.

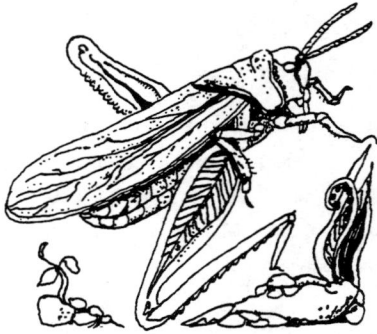

Forest Floor/Herb Layer . . . The forest floor is the habitat of underground insects, microscopic decomposers, worms, snails, and amphibians. Boas and coral snakes find their prey mainly along the forest floor. Coatis normally travel in troops on the forest floor and feed on invertebrates, fruits, nuts, and carrion. Anteaters search for termites. Large spiders seek prey in the leaf litter or on small plants. Larger animals like the ocelot and jaguar also hunt in this layer.

Shrub Layer . . . Extending up to about 3 meters (10 feet), this layer remains relatively dim because little sunlight can filter down through the dense layers above. Lizards and insects are usually plentiful here.

Understory Layer . . . The understory reaches up to about 50 feet and provides a home for animals such as birds, monkeys, tree frogs, vine snakes, and others. Termite nests can be found attached to trees in this layer.

Canopy Layer . . . Reaching up to 100 feet high, the canopy is a thick and rich layer. Monkeys of all kinds—including marmosets, tamarins, spiders, and howlers—as well as lemurs are active here. Toucans, parrots, sloths, and reptiles such as the emerald boa find food in this layer. Bright orchids and bromeliads also compete for space in this region of filtered sunlight. The many insects, snakes, and other animals of this treetop world use lianas as roads to and from this layer.

Emergent Layer . . . At a height of 150 to 200 feet above the forest floor, the emergent layer contains trees that are scattered and do not touch each other. They are like islands in the sky. Butterflies, birds, and certain lizards live in the emergent layer. Harpy eagles swoop down to try to snatch monkeys from the treetops. Insects, snakes, and other predators use the lianas as roads to and from this layer. It is a wild, rainy, and windy environment, but the rain drips down into the forest, leaving this layer relatively drier than those below.

Each creature in each layer is inextricably involved with the others. If we destroy one creature's habitat, the entire ecosystem changes. The rainforest may have 250 species per acre, compared to four or five species per acre in the temperate zone.

Ecosystems ... Ecosystems are self–sustaining natural systems of living things and their non–living physical environment. An ecosystem also includes all of the interactions that form the interconnections and interdependencies among its components. The rainforest ecosystem is complex and fragile. There is fierce competition for food, water, space, and light. Species focus on a narrow band of possible foods and yet have a high number of predators. **Food chains** illustrate a linear relationship between **prey** and **predator**. A piece of vegetation is eaten by a beetle, the beetle is eaten by a frog, and the frog is eaten by a snake. This is a direct chain of events in the predator–prey cycle. However, the vegetation is nibbled on by other invertebrates; the beetle may also be the prey for a spider, toad, snake, or bird; and the snake is dinner for other snakes, birds, and mammals. These interconnected food chains form a **food web**, the representation of the predator–prey cycle within an ecosystem. The basis for most food chains and webs are the **producers**, the green plants that are capable of manufacturing their own food utilizing energy from the sun. **Consumers** are the animals that feed on the green plants and on each other. The decay of dead plant and animal material is the role of the bacteria, yeasts, molds, and fungi—the **decomposers.**

As in many other ecosystems, there is a constant struggle for survival—the daily battle between predator and prey. The rainforest provides a number of examples of protective mechanisms to aid individual animals in surviving: leaf hoppers resemble thorns, walking sticks mimic twigs, moths resemble tree bark, katydids and frogs imitate dead leaves, while snakes counterfeit vines.

People of the Rainforest ... The rainforest can be a rich provider. For centuries, the indigenous peoples of the rainforest have found water, food, and shelter within the boundaries of the forest. Despite the amount of rainfall, water is not easily available in the rainforest because it drips through the leaves and soaks into the ground. Streams and rivers, therefore, must be the major source of water. Food is abundant but difficult to catch. The plant growth is thick and provides hiding places for many animals. People in the rainforest have found it necessary to use a variety of animals for food to supplement their plant diet. This flexibility helps them to survive. Insect larvae and worms are eaten with roots and nuts. A honeycomb is a treat for a whole tribe. Meat is obtained by hunting with bow and arrow, using blowguns, or setting snares and traps. Native peoples also gather medicines from natural sources—roots, bark, leaves, and fungi. Scientists are eagerly investigating this natural pharmacopoeia.

The peoples of the rainforest also construct shelters using rainforest materials. It is usually dark, damp, and warm on the forest floor. The thick canopy layer protects people from harsh storms. However, shelters are still needed. In Zaire, the Pygmies bend branches to the ground and cover rounded huts with large leaves to keep out rain and animals. In Borneo and South America, longhouses are made of branches and palm leaves. Stilts raise these houses off of the jungle floor.

Destruction of the Rainforest... The traditional lifestyles of rainforest peoples are being threatened. The indigenous peoples of the rainforests—perhaps 1000 tribes in all—are finding their hunting, fishing, simple farming, and food gathering cultures disrupted by the loss of animal habitat and native plants, and by the intrusion of other peoples and values. These tribal people themselves are disappearing as diseases are spread, homes are demolished, and new farms, gold mines, and roads fill the former rainforest. The plants and animals of the rainforest are also endangered. Statistics differ as to how quickly the rainforest is disappearing. Some estimate that an area of 72,000 acres (approximately the size of the state of Pennsylvania) is lost per day. Another frequently quoted statistic is that 60 acres are lost every minute, 24 hours a day. At this rate of destruction, by the year 2000, about four million rainforest acres will have been lost and over one million species will have become extinct! Encourage students to think and act postitively and to find out what is being done to prevent the destruction of the rainforest.

Expansion Activities

The activities in this section promote an awareness of the characteristics and interdependencies of the animals in the rainforest. As students explore the adaptations and habitats of rainforest animals, they will discover some of the important interrelationships between living things. They will learn how an animal's body and lifestyle are directly related to its survival. Students will begin to classify animals and plants according to their roles in the rainforest ecosystem.

Activity 1: Adaptation for Survival

materials: large sheet of green construction paper, 8½ x 11 in. sheets of colored paper (green, red, orange, yellow, brown, blue), scissors, tweezers, stopwatch or clock with second hand

Cut out small insect shapes from the colored paper. Be sure to have at least five shapes of each color. Scatter the insects over the large green construction paper (grass field). Have a student use the tweezers (imitating the way a bird uses its beak) and see how many paper insects he or she can pick up in 15 seconds. Record the number picked up for each color. Return all of the caught insect pieces to the grass field. Have students take turns acting as the bird predator and see how many insects they can catch. Record all results. What color insects were caught the most? The least? Why did this happen? What is the advantage of protective colors?

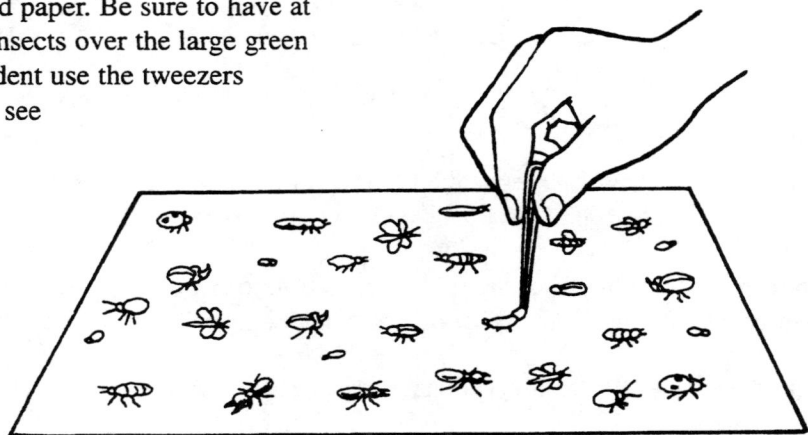

Going Further: Make this activity more challenging by using an artificial grass door mat and broken pieces of colored toothpicks as insects.

Rainforest Log: Enter observations, discoveries, or impressions about adaptations in words, sentences, or drawings.

Activity 2: Habitat Changes

materials: school lawn or weed lot, scissors, four 30 cm (12 in.) rulers, magnifying glass

This activity is designed to determine what effect a change in habitat will have on an animal community.

On a grassy area, form a square with the four rulers. Carefully search the grass for any small organisms such as ants, spiders, moths, pill bugs, worms, or ground beetles. Using a chart like the one shown below, record the kind and number of organisms found. Using the scissors, cut all the grass and other plants in the square. Remove all the clippings. Return to the same area in 24 hours and again carefully search for any organisms. Record the kind and number of organisms found.

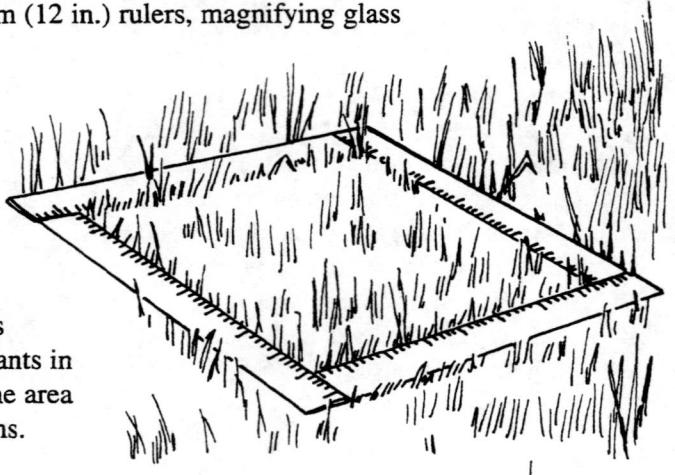

Kind of Organism	Number in Area with Grass	Number in Area without Grass

What kind of organisms were found in the grass? What kinds were the most plentiful? The least plentiful? How many organisms were found the next day in the cut area? What happens when a habitat is destroyed?

Going Further: Check the same area again after thirty days. What changes have taken place? Are the numbers of insects found the same? What do you think happens in a rainforest thirty days after an area has been cleared?

Rainforest Log: Enter observations, discoveries, or impressions in words, sentences, or drawings.

Activity 3: A Jungle Pet

materials: 38–liter (10–gallon) aquarium with lid, gravel, plants (philodendron, fern, ivy) in 4–inch pots, small tree branches, water dish, food dish, American anole lizard

One way to learn more about rainforest animals is to keep one in the classroom as a pet. Anole lizards live in subtropical and tropical rainforests. They are easy to take care of and interesting to watch change colors. Have students research to find out about their living habits and care. Like most lizards, anoles are carnivores and feed on small insects such as mealworms and crickets. Plants in the aquarium should be misted every several days. Anoles may lap up water droplets on plant leaves or drink from a water dish. Do not allow the aquarium to become moist—this encourages mold growth. The floor of the aquarium can be covered with small pieces of gravel. Potted plants and small tree branches will provide climbing places for the lizard. Cover the top of the aquarium with a screen lid. Anoles are fast and can escape if the lid is not properly secured. Observe the actions of the anole. How does it drink water? How does it capture its prey? When does the lizard change color? What colors can it change to? Where does it perch most of the time? If it is a male, observe the action and function of the dewlap, a fanlike fold of skin on the throat. Be sure the students have their rainforest logs handy when they observe the lizard.

Going Further:
1) Help students schedule and determine responsibilities for the pet's needs, including feeding, replenishing water, and cleaning the cage.
2) Ask students to write or illustrate a story about their jungle pet.
3) Find out about the many other kinds of anole lizards in Central and South America.

Rainforest Log: Enter observations and discoveries about the anole or about keeping a pet in general in words, sentences, or drawings.

Activity 4: Creating Rainforest Creatures

In this activity each student will create his or her own rainforest animal, giving it unique body structures, colors, and habits that will allow it to survive in the jungle. The animal might have special body parts or colors to disguise it and prevent it from being caught and eaten. Help students to think in terms of how their jungle creatures will find food and water, capture prey, and protect themselves from rain.

materials: paper, pencils, paint, crayons, colored markers, colored pipe cleaners, glue or transparent tape

In a large group setting, discuss several of the animal adaptations about which students have learned. Provide students with materials to create their creatures. When the creatures have been completed, students can show them to classmates and explain the unique structures, functions, and habits that make their jungle creatures well adapted to the rainforest environment.

Rainforest Log: Find out about special adaptations of these rainforest plants and animals: leaf katydids, ocelots, hoatzins, tapirs, basilisks, marsupial frogs, strangler figs, tree ferns, stilt palms, epiphytes.

Activity 5: Mapping Rainforest Creatures
materials: *Rainforests of the World* (**R**), crayons, butcher paper, pencils, and markers

Each rainforest region has its own unique creatures. African rainforests are home to chimpanzees, gorillas, civets, and Madagascar lemurs. Asian rainforests have the orangutan, black panther, bird of paradise, and hornbill. Central and South American rainforests have even greater numbers of unique creatures, including sloths, toucans, morpho butterflies, poison–arrow frogs, and anacondas. Have students use library resources to find examples of rainforest animals from all the continents. Have students write animal names or draw pictures of the animals in the appropriate areas on their copies of *Rainforests of the World* (**R**). Have students find out if all continents have the following animals in their rainforests: big cats, deer, monkeys or apes, venomous snakes, eagles, and frogs.

Going Further: Create a world map mural using butcher paper and crayons or markers. Draw in the land masses following the outline map of the world as a guide. Mark or color the rainforest areas. Then have students draw in as many of the rainforest animals as they like, each in the appropriate country or region of the world.

An Animal of the Rainforest

The name of my animal is _____.

It lives on the continent of _____.

The color of my animal is _____.

My animal is _____ tall or _____ long.

My animal lives in the _____ layer(s) of the rainforest.

My animal is the predator of _____ or eats

_____.

My animal is the prey of _____ or is afraid of

_____.

My animal is special because _____

_____.

Here is a picture of my creature:

On the back of this paper, draw a picture of your animal in a food chain.

Application of Concepts: *Making Connections*

Portfolios and journals completed by each student provide a profile of observations, discoveries, and impressions about the interactions of living things in the rainforest. Review each student's perceptions and observations to guide the class in pursuing one or more of the activities suggested below. These activities provide the opportunity for each child and the entire class to consolidate their learning of both facts and concepts. Choose a project which gives a sense of understanding, a sense of closure, and a sense of enjoyment to your rainforest group.

Activity 1: Three–Dimensional Mural

materials: recyclable trash (milk jugs, egg cartons, cardboard tubes, wrapping paper, magazines, newspaper), butcher–block paper (preferably green), rainforest plants (African violets, philodendron, and so on), string, masking tape, staplers, crayons, markers, construction paper, tempera paint, brushes

A three–dimensional mural is one major application/presentation project suggested in the section on rainforest fauna. By taking trash such as egg cartons, milk jugs, cardboard, newspaper, string, and so on, the children can make a jaguar, snake, tiny ants, anteaters, or a sloth. What a fun way to recycle! These creatures can be glued onto a mural with a background of jungle vegetation or hung from the ceiling. Be sure to show the layering within the rainforest. Live plants can be placed in the foreground of the mural.

A hallway makes a fine rainforest tunnel. Label each section to illustrate the layers. Each class can concentrate on a single layer and make it a grade–level or school project. The rainforest provides a variety of subjects to explore! Within the classroom, a corner is the best place for a three–dimesional mural. Children will love to sit within it and look up at the wealth of colors and creatures.

Hang large sheets of butcher–block paper from ceiling to floor. Paint in a background of large trees, vines, and so on. See page 17 for making vines and bromeliads. In addition, make your own favorite plants. Place real plants in the forest floor layer. Label the layers. Add creatures for each layer. Populate the mural with drawn or painted creatures, as well as with "stuffed" ones.

materials: white butcher–block paper or newspaper, newspaper or waste paper for stuffing, stapler, markers, crayons, paints and brushes, masking tape, string

To make a "stuffed" creature, first fold a piece of paper in half. Then draw the outline of the whole creature. Decorate it appropriately with paint or markers. Stuff it with newspaper or other waste paper. Staple around the edges and hang it up. Use milk jugs, egg cartons, and so on as bases for other creatures. Decorate authentically.

The mural makes an excellent backdrop for rainforest performances or for the Feast of Tropical Treats (see below). Students can guide guests through the rainforest explaining each creature and how the layers work together in the rainforest ecosystem. Making and then teaching the mural is a good performance–based assessment tool.

Activity 2: Feast of Tropical Treats

Use rainforest foods to create a feast of treats. Invite parents or another class to sample edible products of the jungle. Serve fresh or canned pineapple, Brazil nuts, cashews, tapioca pudding, banana bread, or spice cookies. Warm your guests with cocoa or cool them with fresh fruit juices. The Feast of Tropical Treats gives the children a chance to teach as well as to serve. Entertain your guests with a rainforest rap, read student reports, have guided walks by the mural, or perform a play.

Life in the Rainforest

Activity 3: Measuring Rainforest Destruction

materials: measuring tapes or metersticks; a large, open space (approximately one acre); sidewalk chalk

It is difficult for students to visualize the speed at which the rainforest is being destroyed. One figure states that an acre (an area a little less than a football field) is lost each second. When one considers the diversity of life found within that space, the loss seems even greater.

First, review the causes of rainforest destruction addressed on pages 22–23. Remind students of how important diversity is to the ecosystem. Next, define an acre (4047 square meters or 43,560 square feet). Ask the students to estimate how large the school playground is. Is it bigger than an acre? Smaller than an acre? Record the estimates for later discussion. Review linear measuring skills using metersticks, yardsticks, or tape measures. Measure a square 63.6 meters (208.7 feet) on each side. Have one student stand at each corner and the rest of the class can walk around the square to comprehend the area of an acre. Compare the actual size to the estimates.

Once the area is plotted on the playground, fill it! Use chalk to draw a kapok tree, a jaguar, lianas, monkeys, and other creatures of the jungle. The children will note that they are designing just a flat space; the jungle, however, also has height and depth. It makes for an exhilarating geometry and natural science lesson.

Talk about how long it took to measure the space, to walk it, and to fill it. Discuss how much longer it takes a tree or bird to grow. This representation of an acre of rainforest is lost in the time it takes to snap one's fingers.

Going Further:

1) Make a jungle maze through the acre. Make maps and lead guests through. Charge admission and donate the proceeds to a fund to protect the rainforests.
2) Plan to buy an acre of rainforest through the Rainforest Alliance or the Children's Rainforest. (See *Bibliography*.)
3) How long is a python? Pace out the length of a python (approximately 20 feet). Draw the python and its prey on the playground. Try other predator–prey combinations. How much space do the hunters need?
4) How high is the forest? Ask the custodian how tall the school is and figure out if your school could grow an emergent tree, a canopy tree, etc. How much taller is the emergent layer than your classroom or your school? If you were to cut down the tree and lay it on the playground, would it be longer or shorter than the school?

Activity 4: The Water Cycle

materials: mini jungle terrariums (see page 17) or plastic bag and water

To reinforce the concept of a water cycle, have students write a water cycle chant and practice the polysyllabic words of transpiration, evaporation, and condensation. Add claps for each syllable. Use hand gestures to illustrate the movement of water in the cycle.

If the miniature jungle terrariums have not been used to study the water cycle, place two teaspoons of water in a self–sealing plastic bag. Tape the bag upright to a sunny window area. Observe what happens to the water. Are water droplets seen in the bag? What happens to them? Explain the cycle taking place in the bag.

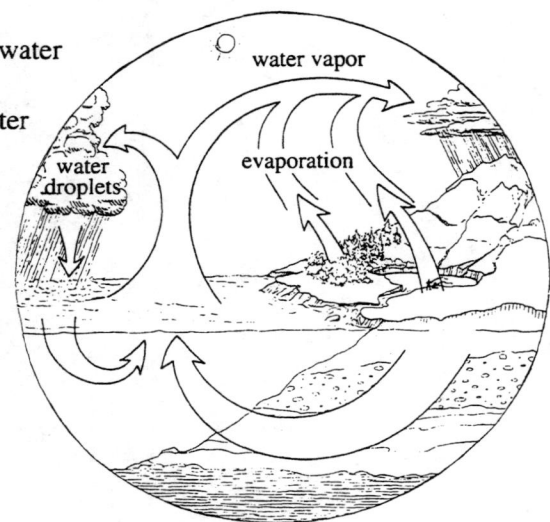

water vapor

water droplets

evaporation

Life in the Rainforest

Activity 5: Create a Rainforest Shelter

With a little research, students can make rainforest shelter models in the classroom. Tribes in the rainforest have their own designs. Rainforest aborigines do not build with brick, stone, or mud; they use readily available materials—branches, leaves, and vines. Some tribes use bent–over branches, tie them with vines, and cover them with large leaves. Other tribes make longhouses of branches raised on stilts. Leaves cover the roof.

Allow students to choose a rainforest shelter to build. Either individually or in pairs, they can design homes which might be found in the jungle. Using materials such as a shoe box or milk carton as a base, they can paste collected leaves and twigs to simulate the building materials. Students can weave materials for making the sides and roofs. Discuss where they will find their food and water. Make small gardens from paper, leaves, and twigs. Label and display.

Have students research the cultures of different continents. Discuss how the inhabitants share food and shelter, and how they work together for protection. Students can write reports or stories about the inhabitants of the rainforest.

Activity 6: Food Chains and Food Webs

For young children, start with a food chain familiar to them. For example, energy from the sun helps a green plant to grow and make food. Cows eat the grass. Meat from the cows is used to make hamburger. Humans eat hamburger: grass—cow—human.

Use words or pictures on individual cards for students to sort and arrange rainforest organisms into a food chain. Example: grass—insect—frog—snake. Have older students create an interconnecting system of food chains to produce a food web typical of a rainforest ecosystem. This food web can be displayed on a bulletin board in the classroom or on a wall in the hallway. Students can label the components and use the display to discuss how each creature is essential to the whole. Talk about variations that might be possible within the web and what effect would be produced if one or more members were removed. What are the advantages and disadvantages of an animal that has only one source of food or one type of prey?

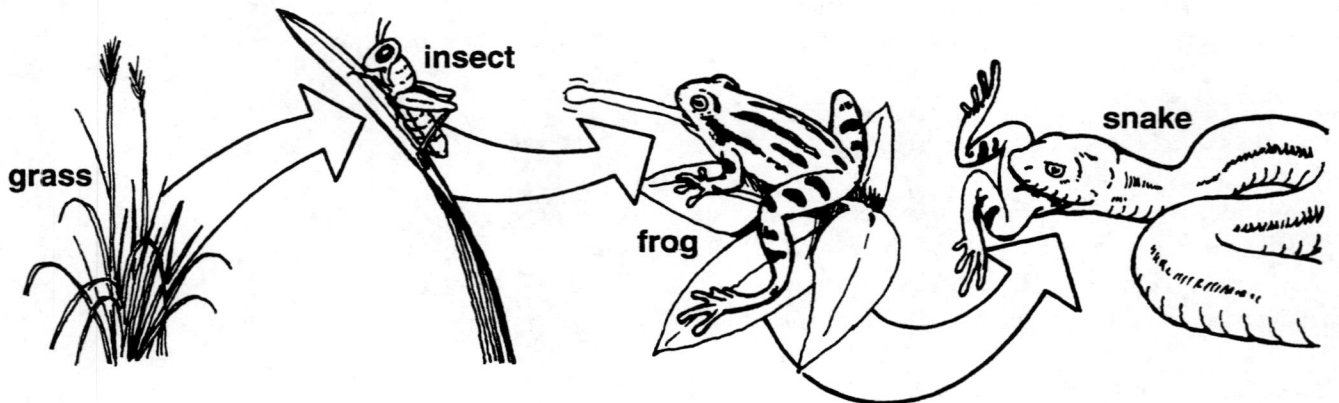

grass   insect   frog   snake

Life in the Rainforest

Activity 7: Size Relationships

Organisms in the rainforest range in size from the very small to the very tall. This activity will help students visualize the comparative sizes of some of the living things in the jungle. Draw lines with chalk on the playground or the side of the school building, or with markers on mural paper to represent the length of such organisms as:

emergent trees	50 m	(165 ft.)
canopy trees	35 m	(115 ft.)
understory trees	15–20 m	(50–65 ft.)
python	9 m	(30 ft.)
anaconda	6 m	(20 ft.)
jaguar (incl. tail)	2.3 m	(7.5 ft.)
gorilla	1.8 m	(6 ft.)
harpy eagle	100 cm	(39 in.)
sloth	50 cm	(18–20 in.)
anole (incl. tail)	15 cm	(6 in.)
toad	7.6 cm	(3 in.)
army ant	1.3 cm	(0.5 in.)

Activity 8: Exploring the Drink of Kings

Cocoa trees are found in the tropical rainforests of Mexico, and Central and South America. The cocoa tree produces a pod–shaped fruit that grows directly from the trunk or branches. Each pod contains 20 to 50 seeds. These seeds are roasted and processed to make cocoa and chocolate. A cocoa drink flavored with spices such as cinnamon was the drink of Aztec and Inca kings. Spanish explorers of the New World brought the drink back with them to Europe.

Show the students cocoa powder. Discuss how the seeds must be removed from the pod and processed to make the premixed cocoa. How many miles did the cocoa product travel from the Tropics to the classroom? What is added to the cocoa powder to make chocolate candy? Prepare a cocoa drink for the students. While the water is heating, use the opportunity to talk about the physical change of the water from a liquid to water vapor, a gas. Watch for bubbles as the water heats. Note the steam. Put a heaping teaspoon of cocoa powder into a cup and add hot water. Stir. Show the students a piece of curled whole cinnamon bark. Allow students to grate the sticks into a coarse powder. Add a pinch of the powder to the drink. Allow the drink to cool until it is safe to drink. How does the drink of kings taste?

Bibliography

FOR CHILDREN

Amsel, Sheri. *Rain Forests*. Austin, TX: Raintree Steck–Vaughn, 1993.

Baker, Lucy. *Life in the Rainforests*. New York: Franklin Watts, 1990.

Cherry, Lynn. *The Great Kapok Tree*. New York: Gulliver Books, 1990.

Cobb, Vicki. *This Place Is Wet*. New York: Walker and Company, 1989.

Dorros, Arthur. *Rain Forest Secrets*. New York: Scholastic, Inc., 1990.

Dunphy, Madeleine. *Here Is the Tropical Rain Forest*. New York: Hyperion Books for Children, 1994.

Forsyth, Adrian. *Journey through a Tropical Jungle*. New York: Simon and Schuster, 1988.

Greenway, Shirley. *Animal Homes: Jungles*. New York: Newington Press, 1991.

Lepthien, Emilie. *Tropical Rain Forest*. Chicago: Children's Press, 1993.

Nations, James D. *Tropical Rainforest: Endangered Environment*. New York: Franklin Watts, 1988.

Ortleb, Edward P. *Jungles: Thematic Unit*. St. Louis: Milliken Publishing, 1995.

Pape, Joyce. *A Closer Look at Jungles*. New York: Gloucester Press, 1978.

Pratt, Kristin Joy. *A Walk in the Rainforest*. Nevada City, CA: DAWN Publications, 1992.

Ross, Suzanne. *What's in the Rainforest?* Los Angeles: Enchanted Rainforest Press, 1991.

Taylor, Barbara. *Rain Forest*. Look Closer Series. New York: Dorling Kindersley, 1992.

FOR TEACHERS

Ayensu, Edward S., editor. *Jungles*. New York: Crown Publishers, 1980.

Bates, Marston. *The Land and Wildlife of South America*. New York: Time–Life Books, 1964.

Collins, M. *The Last Rain Forests*. New York: Oxford University Press, 1990.

Goodman, Billy. *The Rain Forest*. New York: Tern Enterprise, 1991.

Newman, Arnold. *Tropical Rainforest*. New York: Facts on File, 1990.

Perry, Donald. *Life above the Jungle Floor*. New York: Simon and Schuster, 1986.

Ruiz de Larramendi, Alberto. *Tropical Rain Forests of Central America*. Chicago: Children's Press, 1993.

Sanderson, Ivan, with David Loth. *Ivan Sanderson's Book of Great Jungles*. New York: Julian Messner, 1965.

OTHER RESOURCES

COMPUTER/LASER DISC/VIDEO
The Jungle
Humongous Entertainment
CD–ROM for Mac and IBM

The Past and Future Amazon
P. Colinvaux
Scientific American 260 (3), 1990.
Computer/Laser Disc/Video

A Walk in the Rainforest—Belize
Bullfrog Films (Oley, PA)

ORGANIZATIONS

The Children's Rainforest
P.O. Box 936
Lewiston, ME 04240

National Audubon Society
801 Pennsylvania Ave. SE
Washington, DC 20003

National Wildlife Federation
1400 Sixteenth St. NW
Washington, DC 20036-2266

Rainforest Action Network
301 Broadway, Suite A
San Francisco, CA 94133

Smithsonian Tropical Research Institute
APO
Miami, FL 34002-0011